HARVESTERS

By S. M. Maimone

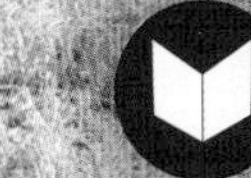

Gareth Stevens
PUBLISHING

Please visit our website, www.garethstevens.com. For a free color catalog of all our high-quality books, call toll free 1-800-542-2595 or fax 1-877-542-2596.

Library of Congress Cataloging-in-Publication Data

Names: Maimone, S. M. (Sofia Maxwell), 1978- author.
Title: Harvesters / S. M. Maimone.
Other titles: Fantastic farm machines.
Description: New York : Gareth Stevens Publishing, [2016] | Series: Fantastic farm machines | Includes index.
Identifiers: LCCN 2016001337| ISBN 9781482445916 (pbk.) | ISBN 9781482445831 (library bound) | ISBN 9781482445718 (6 pack)
Subjects: LCSH: Harvesting machinery–Juvenile literature.
Classification: LCC S695 .M35 2016 | DDC 631.3–dc23
LC record available at http://lccn.loc.gov/2016001337

Published in 2017 by
Gareth Stevens Publishing
111 East 14th Street, Suite 349
New York, NY 10003

Designer: Sarah Liddell
Editor: Therese Shea

Photo credits: Cover, p. 1 My Portfolio/Shutterstock.com; spread background texture used throughout LongQuattro/Shutterstock.com; p. 5 whitehoune/Shutterstock.com; p. 7 Geri Lavrov/Photolibrary/Getty Images; p. 9 Print Collector/Contributor/Hulton Archive/Getty Images; p. 11 ullstein bild/Contributors/ullstein bild/Getty Images; p. 13 (self-propelled) Taina Sohlman/Shutterstock.com; p. 13 (tractor-pulled) PointImages/Shutterstock.com; p. 15 ThomasLENNE/Shutterstock.com; p. 17 Kingcraft/Shutterstock.com; p. 19 Stockr/Shutterstock.com; p. 21 (potato harvester) gillmar/Shutterstock.com; p. 21 (tomato harvester) Kowloonese/Wikimedia Commons; p. 21 (carrot harvester) Konggulerod/Wikimedia Commons.

Printed in the United States of America

CPSIA compliance information: Batch #CS16GS: For further information contact Gareth Stevens, New York, New York at 1-800-542-2595.

CONTENTS

Boldface words appear in the glossary.

Countless Crops

Can you picture yourself picking a field full of crops? On some farms, a field can be so wide and so long that you can't see where it ends. It's a good thing farmers have big machines to help them!

Harvesting by Hand

A harvester is a machine that gathers crops from a field. Before harvesters, people had to gather, or harvest, crops by hand. This took a lot of time and hard work, especially on large farms.

7

Early Harvesters

The reaper was a harvesting machine invented around 1800. It cut crops, but left them in the field. People had to gather and sort the plants into parts they could use. Later reapers swept the plant parts into a box.

9

The first combine harvester was built in 1836. It was pulled by horses. It cut and gathered wheat. It also threshed, which means it sorted the **grain** from the rest of the plant. Later combine harvesters had steam-powered **engines**.

HOLT

Soon, other combine harvesters, or combines, were invented for different kinds of crops. Some were pulled by tractors. Others were self-propelled. That means they had their own engine and could be driven through the fields without a tractor.

self-propelled
tractor-pulled

How It Works

This is how a grain combine harvester works: The front of the combine carries the header. It has a special wheel called a reel that pushes the crop down and into the cutter bar. The cutter bar cuts the crops.

header
cutter bar
reel

The crop is fed onto a **conveyor** and into a threshing drum. The drum shakes the grains from the **stalks**. The grains fall through **sieves** into a tank. The unneeded plant parts, called chaff, are pushed out the machine's back.

When the combine's tank gets full, a tractor with a **trailer** pulls alongside it. An elevator carries the grain up and pushes it out a pipe called an unloader. The grain fills the trailer. The grain is driven somewhere to be stored.

unloader

More Harvesters

Sometimes, combines can use a different header to harvest a different crop. Sometimes, a whole new kind of harvester is needed. Check out these harvesters for carrots, tomatoes, and potatoes. They're fantastic farm machines, too!

carrot harvester
tomato harvester
potato harvester

GLOSSARY

conveyor: a wide, flat, often rubber, band that moves objects from one place to another

engine: a machine that makes power

grain: the seeds of plants such as wheat and corn that are used for food

sieve: a tool with many small holes used to separate small bits of matter from larger ones

stalk: the main stem of a plant that supports other parts

trailer: a cart that is towed by a tractor, truck, or car

FOR MORE INFORMATION

BOOKS

Clay, Kathryn. *Farm Machines.* North Mankato, MN: Capstone Press, 2015.

West, David. *Farm Machinery.* Mankato, MN: Smart Apple Media, 2015.

Wilson, Hannah. *Combine Harvesters.* New York, NY: Kingfisher, 2015.

WEBSITES

Combine Harvesters
www.explainthatstuff.com/howcombineharvesterswork.html
Look at a drawing of the inner workings of a combine harvester.

Wheat Facts
oklahoma4h.okstate.edu/aitc/lessons/extras/facts/wheat.html
Learn about the crop that many kinds of combines harvest: wheat.

Publisher's note to educators and parents: Our editors have carefully reviewed these websites to ensure that they are suitable for students. Many websites change frequently, however, and we cannot guarantee that a site's future contents will continue to meet our high standards of quality and educational value. Be advised that students should be closely supervised whenever they access the Internet.

INDEX